Scottish Book Trust believes that books and reading have the power to change lives. We work with partners throughout the country to inspire, support and challenge the people of Scotland to fulfil their potential as readers and writers and celebrate reading in all its forms.

- We give free books to every child in Scotland to ensure families of all backgrounds can share the joy of books at home.
- We support teachers to inspire children to develop a love of reading, creating innovative classroom activities, book awards and touring authors programme.
- We work with adult learners to tackle social issues and increase literacy skills.
- We nurture and challenge Scotland's writing community by running training, mentoring and awards.
- We fund a range of author events for the public to enjoy and promote Scottish writing to people worldwide.

www.scottishbooktrust.com

WALK THE WALK

Written by Gowan Calder

Illustrated by Jill Calder

www.scottishbooktrust.com

First published in 2014 in Great Britain by
Scottish Book Trust, Sandeman House, Trunk's Close,
55 High Street, Edinburgh EH1 1SR, Scotland, UK
Reprinted 2015, 2016

In partnership with the Scottish Government
© Crown Copyright 2014

ISBN 978-1-901077-28-5   Free

Script by Gowan Calder
Illustrations and cover art by Jill Calder
Typeset by 3btype.com

Printed and bound in Poland, EU by Drukarnia POZKAL, Inowrocław

www.scottishbooktrust.com

www.scottishbooktrust.com/walkthewalk

Contents

Foreword

Welcome to *Walk The Walk*, an interactive graphic novel for use in facilitated youth and literacy-support groups. *Walk The Walk* was developed by Scottish Book Trust, in partnership with the Scottish Government, to explore issues around sectarianism and how to tackle it. The story follows one day in the lives of two best friends: Rab McGowan and Robbie Black. It's the day that Rab's cousin Kylie is supposed to marry Robbie's brother Romeo, but there are people at both ends of The Walk who don't want the wedding to happen. As the two families face up to their shared past, can Rab and Robbie convince their grans to put their differences aside for just one day?

You will find 'jump-off points' throughout this book, indicating opportunities for discussion about a particular aspect of the book's story, or its wider themes. Each of these jump-off points is marked by a symbol and links to one of the many online supporting activities, which you can download for FREE at **www.scottishbooktrust.com/walkthewalk.**

At the back of this book you will find What Happens Next?, a supporting activity that enables learners to come up with their own ideas for how each character's story might progress. There is also a glossary that explains the meanings of some of the words used in the story.

At **www.scottishbooktrust.com/walkthewalk** you will also find a PDF version of *Walk The Walk*, which will allow you to listen to the story being read out loud, or increase the size of the text to help you read it.

There are also links to other relevant websites.

Tutors' Frequently Asked Questions

We would like every learner and tutor to enjoy reading and re-reading *Walk The Walk*. We hope that the answers to these frequently asked questions will help you to get the most out of using the resource.

1. Who is *Walk The Walk* for?

Walk The Walk is a graphic novel for learners aged sixteen and above who struggle with literacy. It was created using Scottish Book Trust's custom methodology, and literacy learners were involved in the research, pilot and control stages of the book's development. However, *Walk The Walk* can also be used with other learner groups, including reluctant readers and youth groups.

2. I've never talked about sectarianism with my group before: can I still use this book?

Walk The Walk is designed to enable all tutors to discuss the subject of sectarianism in their learner groups with confidence. Each of our learner activities is accompanied by an in-depth tutor support note, and each activity is structured in a way that encourages self reflection as well as group discussion. In addition, a glossary is provided so tutors can help learners get to grips with any words or terms that may be new to them, and a list of useful websites for further reading is provided at the back of this book and online: **www.scottishbooktrust.com/walkthewalk**.

3. How should I read *Walk The Walk* with my group?

The best way to read *Walk The Walk* is aloud, in a group setting. We have discovered that even shy learners really enjoy reading different characters out loud and getting into the role. The characters in *Walk The Walk* have been specifically developed to allow all learners to get involved. The sentences are short, familiar dialects are used throughout, and an activity to help learners familiarise themselves with the pronunciation of characters' names is included at the beginning. A learner who is very confident reading aloud can choose a character with more lines (like Gran or Robbie), while a learner who is less confident can choose a character with only a few lines (like Karen or Johnny). Learners who don't feel confident to read aloud also benefit from hearing the lines brought to life by other readers as they follow the action via the book's illustrations. There are additional benefits: as research shows, 'repeated reading' is one way of improving both reading speed and comprehension. What better way to make this process engaging than to rehearse a script, reading it aloud together and performing it?

4. What if none of my learners want to read aloud?

We know that reading aloud can be daunting. However, whenever we trial our graphic novels with learners, we discover that once they hear others reading aloud, they become more keen to get involved. During the development of this book, groups enjoyed adopting different accents and voices, illustrating increased enjoyment and confidence in reading aloud. If your group is hesitant, we suggest reading the first few pages aloud yourself – perhaps with help from another staff member – so your learners can get used to the reading level.

5. How long does it take to read through *Walk The Walk*?

Different groups of learners read at different speeds and with varying levels of confidence. However, we have found that the book can be read in two two-hour sessions. Additional time should be built in to complete the supporting activities.

6. What level of support will my learners require to complete the activities?

Different activities require different levels of tutor input. In the tutor support notes for each activity, we have given an indication of the amount of support learners may require.

7. Is *Walk The Walk* suitable for learners whose first language is not English?

Yes. We hope that a wide variety of learners will find *Walk The Walk* accessible and engaging. We have provided a glossary at the back of the book, which learners can refer to if they're unsure about certain words or phrases. We have also created a learner activity that allows learners to get to know the names and faces of the book's characters before they start reading. This activity is called What's In A Name? and it includes an accompanying support note for tutors: www.scottishbooktrust.com/walkthewalk.

8. Where can I find out more about *Walk The Walk*?

You can find all our tutor support notes and learner activities, and download a PDF copy of *Walk The Walk*, at our website. The website also contains more information about *Walk The Walk*, and about Scottish Book Trust's other Adult Learning projects. www.scottishbooktrust.com/walkthewalk.

9. Where can I find the *Walk The Walk* tutor support notes and learner activities?

We have included a selection of learner activities in the back of the book itself. However, you can find a whole suite of tutor support notes and learner activity ideas at our website: **www.scottishbooktrust.com/walkthewalk**.

10. How do I use the support notes and learner activities?

As you read through *Walk The Walk*, you will notice symbols at the bottom of select pages. These are points at which we recommend you stop reading to facilitate discussion with your group and complete some activities. To help you, we have provided discussion questions for each of these jump-off points. We have also created support notes to guide tutors through each activity, and activity sheets for learners to complete. All the activities are designed to build on the learners' progress through the book, and to complement each other – so if you can, we'd recommend completing all the activities in a sequential order.

Additional Support Materials

The additional support materials, which further explore the issues and themes included in the story, are:

What's In A Name?
Allows learners to get to know the names and faces of the book's characters, and to practice pronunciation, before they start reading

You Are Here
Focuses on sense of place and possible barriers to creating a safe community

Social Media
Explores aspects of social networking, and the role it can play in combating sectarian behaviour

Songs and Chants
Raises awareness of sectarianism in popular culture, with particular reference to songs and sporting chants

Then and Now
Promotes intergenerational discussion about the changing face of sectarianism and identity in Scotland

Belonging and Identity
Encourages learners to reflect on the places and groups to which they belong

All Colours
Explores the symbolism behind different colours, both in relation to sectarianism and in a wider sense

What Happens Next?
Considers the various ways in which we can all take responsibility for tackling sectarianism

The McGowans

GRAN

Therese McGowan is known as Therese or Mrs McGowan on The Walk and is called 'Gran' by her grandchildren Rab, Weezee, Malkie and Kylie.

MICK

Mick is Gran's eldest son and Rab and Weezee's dad.

Eileen is Kylie and Malkie's mum, she is separated from Gran's other son, who works on the rigs.

EILEEN

WEEZEE

Weezee is short for 'Wee Louise'. She is Rab's little sister and deaf but that never stops her!

RAB

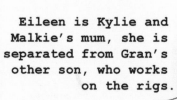

Rab is 21, he works for the Council and he loves his girlfriend and son.

KYLIE

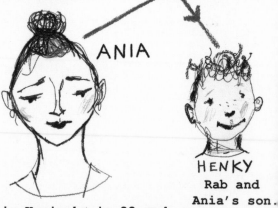

ANIA

HENKY
Rab and Ania's son.

MALKIE

Malkie is 24 and a bit of a 'bad boy' on The Walk.

Kylie is 23 and about to get married.

Ania Kaminska is 23 and is Rab's Polish girlfriend.

Back in the 1980s...

THERESE McGOWAN (GRAN)

SANDY
An old pal of Mick McGowan's.

On The Walk...

MIREMBE

FATHER O'BRIEN

Mirembe is originally from Rwanda in Africa but moved to The Walk with her Scottish husband.

A local priest and family friend.

The Blacks

EH?

WHAT'S IN A NAME?

MARGARET BLACK (NAN)

Margaret is called 'Mags' by most folk on The Walk and 'Nan' by Robbie and Romeo.

KAREN

Karen divorced Johnny ten years ago and has remarried but she loves her sons, Romeo and Robbie.

JOHNNY

Johnny is also known as 'The Man in Black'.

ROBBIE

Robbie is 21. He is Rab's best friend and at university.

ROMEO

Romeo is 26 and is about to get married to Kylie.

REVEREND SCOTT

ie local minister.

MR LEVIN

Mr Levin's family were refugees from Germany in 1938. He has lived on The Walk almost all his life. He is a widower.

Back in the 1980s...

MAGS BLACK (NAN)

JOHNNY BLACK

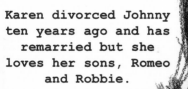

Walk The Walk

On The Walk — a young man walks towards us, walks past us, stops, walks back... looks at us.

Rab: Hiya, awright? Here for the wedding are you? Bride or groom's side?

He spots Robbie on the other side of The Walk. Robbie spots him too and waves.

Rab: Aye, aye — here's trouble...

Rab crosses the street.

Robbie: Rab, ma man — good to see you! All ready for the big day, eh...?

Robbie spots us.

Robbie: Who's yer pals?

Rab: Strangers to this land, Robbie.

Robbie: Oh, so needing the tour are you? Bride or groom? Or should I say 'Tap End' or 'Bottom End'?

Rab: I've told you, Robbie — they're no' from around here.

Robbie: Well what should I say? What foot do you kick with? Bluenose or Tim? Billy Boy or Feee—

Rab: Robbie! Let's not use the 'F' word around our guests. Where are yer manners?

Robbie: Pardon me. Welcome to The Walk, eh? Whoever you are!

Rab: This is my old pal, Robert 'Robbie' Black.

Robbie: And this is *my* old pal, Robert 'Rab' McGowan.

Rab: Known each other since the first day of primary school, but.

Robbie: Aye – you broke ma nose.

Rab: You chucked a brick at me! Still got the scar...
           but we were just being wee laddies, eh?

Robbie: Both up in front of the Heidy... he said he
           wished they still had the belt.

Rab: You laughed.

Robbie: I did – still had the belt in my house.

Rab: Aye, mine too.

Robbie: One hundred lines for our punny eccy. *'I will not
           throw bricks at other peeple.'*

Rab: *'I will not break other peeple's noses.'*

Robbie: I still canny spell 'peeple'.

Rab: Aye – me neither!

Robbie: Firm friends since, but.

Rab: Aye, firm friends.

Robbie: Old Firm friends, you might say.

Rab: Even though it got tricky when we went to different
           high schools.

Robbie: Had to pretend we were mortal enemies...

Rab: Aye – running battles in the back field...

Robbie: Had to knock you about a bit, eh?

Rab: Get tae! Mair like the other way around...

Robbie: Let's not start, eh? Leave it to the others...

Rab: Aye. Good point, well made. So – this is where we
          grew up... Meadow Walk.

Robbie: No' a meadow now, but. Just The Walk.

Rab: And it's where we walk... *Some* with fife and drums.
          Some just out for a stroll...

Robbie: *Some* for a victory march, eh?

Rab: Hey Robbie, what time is it?

Robbie: Don't start...

Rab: Five-two, five-two. FIVE. TWO... Get it up ya!

Robbie: Aye, whatever.

Rab: Just a bit of banter, eh, pal?

Robbie: Wish it was, pal, but it goes deeper than that.

Rab: Aye, sorry.

They both look at us.

Rab: See, I'm from the Tap End o' The Walk.

Robbie: And I'm from the Bottom End, and it feels like
          we've been at war forever.

Rab: '*Two households baith alike in dignity...*'

Robbie: Eh?

Rab: '*From ancient grudge break to new mutiny*'... aye?

Robbie: Naw. Have you lost it?

Rab: '*From forth the fatal loins of these two foes
          A pair of star-crossed lovers take their life.*'

Robbie: Do I know you?

YOU ARE HERE

Rab: Shakespeare, pal. *Romeo and Juliet*. What dae they
            teach you at university, eh?

Robbie: That'll be Applied Mathematics, *pal*. I saw that
            film, but. Leonardo DiCaprio, aye?

Rab: That's the one. Just saying – this wedding is pure
            dead *Romeo and Juliet,* naw?

Robbie: Well, Romeo and Kylie, aye.

Rab: Aye – your brother, Romeo Black.

Robbie: And your cousin, Kylie McGowan.

Rab: No' a popular choice in this neighbourhood. A lot
            of bad blood between our families...

Robbie: I hear your cousin Malkie is out of Bar-l and
            coming home for the big day.

Rab: *I* heard your dad has strolled into town 'n' aw.

Robbie: Aye. There's gonnae be trouble. My nan is holding
            a war council down our end.

Rab: Aye, my gran up our end too. Here we go again, eh?

Weezee appears out a door, waves at the boys.

Robbie: Hey, it's Wee Louise! Hiya Weezee!

Weezee signs something to Rab.

Robbie: What did she say?

Rab: She says '*Hiya, Bluenose'.*

Robbie: She did not... did she? Do they really have a sign
            for that?

Rab: She's deaf, Robbie, no' an alien. That's the sign
          for a Rangers supporter, apparently.

Robbie: No shit? I heard your lot have a different sign
          language from us.

Rab: What d'ye mean by 'your lot'? The McGowan family?
          Celtic Football Club...? *Catholics?*

Robbie: Naw – you know what I mean...

Rab: There *are* different ways of signing things,
          awright? But she's no' using some *secret* code!

Robbie: Awright, calm doon... Weezee started it!

Rab: She's twelve, Robbie, and deaf. She's never *heard*
          the banter, it's just signs and words to her.

Robbie: That's where it starts, Rab. With words.

They glare at each other for a moment, fists ready.

Robbie: I'd better go. I'm expected at my nan's.

Rab: Aye, me and Weezee are expected at my auntie's.
          Time to part ways, eh?

Robbie: Aye... But I wouldn't hurt a hair on Weezee's
          head, Rab, and I'd lamp anyone that tried.

Rab: I know that. Firm friends, eh?

Robbie: Firm friends. Catch you later at the tree...

WORDS

Rab and Weezee set off down The Walk. Rab stops, looks back at us.

Rab: Well, are you coming or no'? Might as well meet
           the family... And speak of the devil!

Rab's girlfriend Ania arrives with their son, Henky.

Rab: Hiya, pal! How was nursery?

Ania: Someone was on the naughty step, weren't you?

Rab: Henrik Marek 'Larsson' McGowan, what did you do?

Ania: Rab - I've told you not to call him that!

Rab: Sorry, love... It's just my wee joke, eh?

Ania: Well this is *serious*. A wee boy called him a bad
           word so Henky whacked him one.

Rab: Well, what did the other boy call him?

Ania: He won't tell me - but Henky knows that you don't
           hit people, Rab.

Rab: Aw c'mon, Ania. Does it no' depend...?

Ania: No. NO hitting. That's the rule, isn't it, Rab...?
           ISN'T IT, RAB?

Rab: Aye, okay! Your mum's right, Henky. No hitting.

Ania: The other boy got the naughty step too.

Rab: Aye, well, good. Wonder what he said though?

Ania: Something bad he learnt at home, probably.

Rab: Sounds like his dad needs the naughty step too.

Ania: (*whispers*) I think his dad is in the jail.

...YOU COMING OR NO'?

Rab: Aw – the BIG naughty step, eh?

Weezee is watching some women on the other side of The Walk.
She tugs Rab's sleeve and signs something.

Rab: Do you know those lassies over there, Ania?

Ania: Yeah, I've seen them about.

Rab: Weezee says they're bitching about you.

Ania: And how do you know that *Detective* McGowan?

Weezee signs to Rab again.

Rab: She says, '*Very funny, Ania. I'm deaf, I'm no'*
          blind.'

Ania: They're just peed off because Henky got a place at
          the nursery.

Rab: Eh? Why? No' because you're Polish?

Ania: Mebbe. They think they reserve the places
          specially for the *Catholics*.

Rab: That's nuts! He was a January baby...

Ania: Exactly. And I'm organised. It's our way. I didn't
          want to be a *kura domowa.*

Rab: Oh, I love it when you talk dirty...

Ania: It's not dirty! It's a... I think you say, home
          chicken?

Rab: Aye? What's a 'home chicken' when it's at home?

Ania: A lady who just cleans the house and cooks and
          looks after the pig-husband and the kids...

Rab: Sounds great to me...

Ania: Then you need a new girlfriend! You'd never get
           to your precious football if I didn't work!

Rab: I know, I know... I was only kidding!

*Ania stomps off with Henky. Weezee holds up her hand and
pretends to blow a whistle.*

Rab: Aye, I know. I've been shown the red card.

Rab and Weezee set off. A woman comes out of her door.

Mrs Ross: Robert, come here a minute!

Rab: Hiya, Mrs Ross. You alright?

Mrs Ross: Aye fine. You still working for the council?

Rab: Aye – road department, paving an' that.

Mrs Ross: I've got a wee 'homer' for you. Ma pal down the
           Bottom End wants her lawn mono-blocking.

Rab: Oh aye, canny be bothered mowing, eh?

Mrs Ross: Naw – her husband says the lawn's too *green*.

Rab: Are you joking?

Mrs Ross: No. Will you do it or no'? Cash in hand...

Rab: Aye, well – I could use the money, like.

Mrs Ross: Only thing is, you have to do it when her man's
           away so he doesn't know you're a McGowan...

Rab: I'll go in disguise, eh? See, I'm saving for an
           engagement ring for Ania so it's worth it.

He looks at Weezee, they look at us.

Rab: Only on 'The Walk'... Mad, eh?

Robbie is walking towards the Bottom End. He sees us.

Robbie: You still here, eh? Come and meet my neighbour!

He stops outside Mirembe's house. We can see into her front room. She spots us and waves.

Robbie: I know what you're thinking: *'she's no' from around here...'*

Mirembe opens her window and leans out.

Mirembe: You talking about me, Robbie?

Robbie: Aye, I'm saying you're not from these parts.

Mirembe: Right... I'm from Edinburgh!

Robbie: We know. You're the only one on The Walk with no net curtains. Happy to let folk look right in!

Mirembe: Why not? I like my house. I think it looks nice.

Robbie: It's like an art gallery, wi' all those statues.

Mirembe picks up a wooden doll and shows it to Robbie.

Mirembe: My sister sent me a new one. Isn't she beautiful? She is an Acua'ba. A fertility doll.

Robbie: Oh aye?

Mirembe: My sister gave it to me because me and Jimmy are trying to make babies.

Robbie: Oh man – too much information, Mirembe!

Mirembe: Why? I am proud of my culture. Aren't you proud of your culture, Robbie? And your history?

Robbie: Some of it, aye.

Mirembe: Then open your curtains and show us!

Robbie: There's some bad stuff too, Mirembe. Stuff I'm not
            so proud of but canny seem to lose.

Mirembe: Oh, me too, but I chose to walk away from that.

Robbie: Hard to walk away when it's family...

Mirembe: (*quietly*) Hey, who is that man over there?

*Robbie looks over. Malkie is sitting on a low garden wall,
rolling a cigarette. He is watching them.*

Robbie: That's Malkie. Rab's cousin. He was a couply years
            above us in the school.

Mirembe: He looks *mean*.

Robbie: Aye maybe. Never used to be. He was everybody's
            golden boy back then. Top marks in the school.

Mirembe: Doesn't look 'golden' to me.

Robbie: Rab says it all went Pete Tong when he was about
            thirteen.

Mirembe: Pete Tong is 'wrong', right?

Robbie: Aye. He got his first season ticket for Parkhead
            and started getting in aw sorts of trouble.

Mirembe: Fighting?

Robbie: That kindy thing, aye.

Mirembe: Tribal warfare, eh? That's what I had to get away
            from.

Robbie: And that's why we have to keep our curtains
            closed.

His phone rings. He answers it.

Robbie: Aye, aye... I know, Nan! I'm coming...

Rab and Weezee reach their Auntie Eileen's.

Rab: Here we are. Home of the Mother of the Bride.

Weezee pulls a monstrous face!

Rab: Aye, you're right. Ma-zilla of the Bridezilla!

Eileen opens the door.

Eileen: Robert McGowan, get yourself in here NOO! Where
            have you been? Your gran's going mental...

*They go into the front room. Kylie is sitting on the sofa,
her hair in massive curlers.*

Kylie: Gran's pure rantin', Rab. She's saying she'll no'
            come to the wedding.

Rab: How bad is it? Is she singing the songs?

Kylie: Aye. You know what that means.

Rab: Aye. You've got to take cover when she starts on
            the Irish songs...

Kylie: Then it's all – *'You dinnae know!'*

Rab: *'You werny there!'*

Kylie: *'They were dark days, dark days indeed...'*

Rab: *'We were dirt poor... blah, blah... Your granda
            couldny get a job 'cause he was Irish... blah.'*

Eileen: Don't you be cheeky about your granny! That woman
            raised you, Rab McGowan!

Rab: Aye, I know but it's all ancient history...

Eileen: What do you know? You *weren't* there.

Rab: Is it no' time to just get over it?

34

Eileen: It goes both ways, Rab. Show him Kylie.

Rab: Show me what?

Weezee is looking at Kylie's iPad. She gives it to Rab.

Kylie: Someone posted this on Romeo's Facebook.

It is an old black and white sign. Rab reads it.

Rab: *No Blacks. No Dogs. No Irish.* Who the hell posted
           that?

Weezee signs 'Bluenose'.

Kylie: Don't do that, Weezee. It's not a Rangers fan.
           It's just some ignorant chav...

Rab: Who wrote this? *'Romeo, why are you marrying that
           Irish dog?'*

Kylie: His ex-girlfriend. She's just jealous.

Rab: (*quietly*) I can see why Gran is angry...

Kylie: Leave it, Rab.

Rab: I'm ragin' myself...

Kylie: Don't. I love Romeo, he loves me. We're getting
           married and folk need to get over it.

Rab: Have you seen this other stuff on his page...?

Kylie: Aye - it's just banter. I bet you say the same
           about Rangers.

Rab: Naw...! Aye, well... Maybe - but it's more funny
           stuff, like...

Kylie: If you want to do something, go and talk to Gran.
           I want her at my wedding, Rab.

Rab: Aye. Aye, okay. But I'm still ragin'.

Rab and Weezee are back on The Walk. A group of women are gossiping in a front garden. They wave 'hullo'.

Rab: That's the thing about The Walk. Everybody knows everybody. Which is good... and bad.

Malkie is swaggering down the street. He spots Rab and Weezee. Rab grabs Weezee by the arm.

Rab: Go to Gran's, okay? I'll see you there.

Weezee: (*crosses her arms and shakes her head*)

Rab: I mean it, Weezee. NOW.

Weezee flicks him the 'V's and walks off.

Malkie: Robert.

Rab: Malcolm.

Malkie: Good to see ya. Was that Wee Louise just there? She's grown up, eh?

Rab: You've been away a while, Malkie. Things change.

Malkie: Aye, true enough. So, are ye ready?

Rab: Well, Kylie's sitting in her onesie wi' curlers on, but the rest of us are sorted.

Malkie: I'm no' talking about the wedding.

Rab: That's all that's happening here the day, like.

Malkie: The Man in Black is in town.

Rab: Aye. Johnny Black is the father of the groom, Malkie. He'll want to be at his son's wedding.

Malkie: Maybe. But I think he's here to start something.

Rab: Well he can start it on his own and finish it on his own. Romeo's a pal and Robbie's a *good* pal.

Malkie: And do you think The Man in Black gives a toss
            about your wee bromance wi' his son?

Rab: For God's sake, Malkie - Kylie's your sister!
            Can you no' put this shite aside for one day?

Malkie: I'm no' looking for trouble, Rab. I'm just saying
            I'm ready.

*He pulls something out of his jacket. There is a glint of
steel in the sunshine.*

Rab: You must be jokin' me? Are you mad? Did you learn
            nothing in the jail?

Malkie: I learned this is war, Rab, ma boy. And I'm ready
            for battle. So I'm asking you, are *you* ready?

Rab: I'm ready for a wedding, no' a funeral.

Malkie: I canny help wondering whose side you're on...

Rab: I'm no' taking sides.

Malkie: Gran will be disappointed you've no' got your
            family's back.

Rab: Don't bring Gran into this...

Malkie: She's already in it, pal. See you later.

Malkie walks off. Rab calls after him.

Rab: Malkie...! I've got your back, okay? I've got your
            back.

Malkie: Good man.

Malkie walks off singing.

Malkie: *'When you walk in a storm, hold your head up high
            and don't be afraid of the dark...'*

Malkie saunters down The Walk. He stops at a bush and speaks to it.

Malkie: Alright, Weezee? I can see you in there. I'm no' Inspector Taggart but I've got *eyes,* eh?

Mr Levin comes out his front door. Sees Malcolm.

Levin: Well, if it's not the prodigal son.

Malkie: Hullo Mr Levin. Shalom! Peace be with you, right?

Mr Levin nods and continues walking, looking worried. He passes Rab sitting on a wall with his head in his hands.

Levin: Hello, Robert — you alright there?

Rab: Oh hi, Mr Levin. Just taking a wee break.

Levin: Busy day, eh? I'm looking forward to the wedding. It was nice of Kylie to invite me.

Rab: You're a legend on The Walk, Mr Levin.

Levin: Well, I've been here a long time — man and boy. I've watched you all grow up.

Rab: Kylie says you're like everybody's granda. You remember everything about everyone.

Levin: Aye, I mind seeing you in your school play. *Romeo and Juliet,* wasn't it? Who were you again?

Rab: Mercutio, Romeo's pal.

Levin: That's right. I remember you were very good at the sword fighting.

Rab: Not that good. I ended up dead.

Levin: Well, that's the trouble with *Romeo and Juliet,* eh? Everybody winds up deid.

The Walk is quiet. Weezee comes out of hiding, sees Johnny Black marching down the middle of the road and hides again. The Man in Black is singing.

Johnny: '*My father wore it as a youth in bygone days of yore, and on the Twelfth I love to wear...*'

Robbie comes tearing after him.

Robbie: Dad! Dad – shut the hell up will you? We can hear you clear down the Bottom End.

Johnny: '*For those brave men who crossed the Boyne...*'

Robbie: SHUT IT! I mean it. Have some respect for our neighbours.

Johnny: I do, son. I'm just singing. Singing an old traditional song.

Robbie: It's not the song and you know it. It's what you *mean* by singing it.

Johnny: Time was, you were happy to sing it with me.

Robbie: I was a wee boy, Dad. I thought I was part of something. Part of history.

Johnny: And so you were, son. Mind what we called ourselves? The Black and Blue and Orange Men...

Robbie: I remember, Dad.

Johnny: We had T-shirts made up. Singing on the terraces wi' our special T-shirts – what a laugh.

Robbie: I'm no' laughing now.

Johnny: Naw – I heard you've got a right soor pus since you've been up at the university.

Robbie: I learned what you were up to well before then.

Johnny: And what about the McGowans, eh?

Robbie: I know what Rab's *dad* did, aye. But that family has more than paid for it.

Johnny: I canny believe you hang about with that wee toerag Rab...

Robbie: I can. We have the same name, same mental grannies and the same waster dads...

Johnny: And that your brother is marrying a McGowan...

Robbie: Same street we grew up on...

Johnny: A bloody McGowan!

Robbie: Are you listening, Dad? We are THE SAME!

Johnny: And what about Malkie. Is *he* your pal?

Robbie: No. No he's naw.

Johnny: Because that boy's looking for trouble. Your brother knows it.

Robbie: He'll no' find it here. Romeo's getting married in less than two hours and I'm gonnae be there.

Johnny: And where exactly is that, son? On which side?

Robbie: By my brother's side. I'm his best man.

Johnny: Whatever happens?

Robbie: Whatever happens, Dad. I'm always his best man.

Johnny: Good. We'll need you when it all kicks off.

Robbie: If.

Johnny: When, son, *when*.

Weezee comes out of the shadows. She looks at us, she signs, 'I've got eyes'.

Rab arrives at his gran's house. He looks at us.

Rab: I'm warning you, Therese McGowan is a bit o' a
           nutter. Mair Irish than a leprechaun...

He walks into the front room. Gran is cleaning furiously.

Rab: ...even though she was born in East Kilbride.

Gran: And where on God's earth have *you* been?

Rab: Up at Auntie Eileen's...

Gran: So you've heard. I'll no' be caught deid at that
           wedding, whatever you've come to say.

Rab: Kylie really wants you there, Gran. That's all.

Gran: Well, I was gonnae go, seeing as Romeo agreed to
           get married in St Joseph's. But no' now.

Rab: I saw what they wrote on Facebook, Gran and I'm
           ragin' too. But it wasn't Romeo who wrote it.

Gran: Naw, it was his Billy Boy pals.

Rab: If they were his pals, they won't be now. They
           took it too far and he'd do anything for Kylie.

Gran: If she'd any sense she'd walk away now...

Rab: She trusts him, Gran. She loves him.

Gran: Aye, well, a fish can love a bird but where would
           they live?

Rab: In a tree house wi' a swimming pool? C'mon, Gran,
           it's the twenty-first century, you can marry who
           you want!

Gran: Am I supposed to forget the past?

Rab: No – but let's leave it in the past and move on.

Gran: When my mother came from Ireland in 1923 she cleaned house for the local minister.

Rab: He was a nice man, eh? He taught her to read.

Gran: So he did and when she got good at it she read everything she could get her hands on...

Rab: Aye, I mind her reading me stories when I was wee.

Gran: Until she found that paper on his desk. *The Menace of the Irish Race*... Was he a *nice* man?

Rab: He still employed her and it was a long time ago...

Gran: In *1960* your grandfather went for a job in the bank and got telt to his face he wouldn't go far...

Rab: Maybe he wasn't good at counting?

Gran: So he ended up in the shipyards where he got telt every day to '*go home, ya dirty fenian...*'

Rab: Things have changed, Gran. You canny do that now.

Gran: Really? Well someone forgot to tell the lassie who called my granddaughter an *Irish dog*!

Rab: We've got to rise above it, Gran, for Kylie's sake.

Gran is scrubbing away at her coffee table.

Gran: To think, I let that filthy Romeo Black in my house...!

Rab: Listen to yourself, Gran! That's no' *nice* either!

Gran: And I will never forgive what *they* did to your da.

Rab: Dad made his own choices and he has to live with them.

Gran: YOU WEREN'T THERE! Johnny Black started it...

May 10th, 1980 in the Walk Inn pub. It is the night of the Old Firm Scottish Cup Final. Gran is there with some other locals. Her son, Mick McGowan, bursts in.

Mick: '*Hail, Hail the Celts are here!*'

Gran: Was it a good game, son?

Mick: It wasnae bad. Mick Conroy pulled a blinder and McCluskey was pure gold!

Gran: We heard there was a wee bit o' trouble?

Mick: '*A wee bit o' trouble*'? Brilliant! It was a full-scale riot, Ma. Polis on horses... the lot!

Gran: Tell me you weren't involved, son.

Mick: Well, after the whistle a few of us stormed the pitch to salute our boys. All good clean fun...

Gran: If you say so. Sounds daft to me.

Mick: Next thing we know the Rangers fans are on the pitch too and it's raining bottles...!

Gran: I've always said you shouldn't have drink at the matches. You're lucky you weren't hurt...

Gran walks off, shaking her head.

Mick: The Battle of Hampden! *What* a day, eh lads? Best two quid I ever spent.

A group of lads wearing Rangers scarves enter the bar.

Mick: Oy, oy – *Hunny*, we're home! I believe you owe me a pint, Sandy, old pal?

Sandy: Aye, fair enough. Enjoy it, Mickey, my boy, because you'll be buying next year.

Mick: No chance! You get out okay, mate?

Sandy: I nearly got scalped by a bottle of Bucky but I got out before the polis charged, aye.

They drink together. Gran starts to climb onto a table.

Sandy: Mrs McGowan, please dinnae rub it in!

Gran: You know the Walk Inn rules, son. The victors choose the song. I love this new one...

Mick: Aw dinnae, Ma. They've had a bad day already...

Gran: (*sings*) *'By a lonely prison wall I heard a young girl calling...'*

Mick: Seriously, Ma – dinnae start.

Gran: *'Michael they are taking you away...'*

Sandy: There's no harm in it, Mick. It's a good song.

Johnny Black appears out of a dark corner.

Johnny: The Irish blaming the British as usual!

Gran: *'For you stole Trevelyn's corn...'*

Johnny: Somebody shut her up.

Gran: *'So the young could see the morn...'*

Johnny: Shut the old cow up!

Mick: What did you say?

Sandy: Leave it, Mick. Don't rise to it.

Johnny: Is that old slag still singing?

Mick punches Johnny and before anyone knows what's happening glasses are flying and war is waging...

MAY 10th, 1980

WALK·INN

DEAD

*We are back in the present day. Gran has stopped cleaning
and is sitting, defeated, on the sofa.*

Gran: The lads were full of booze and overexcited efter
         the match. You know how it is.

Rab: Aye, even without the booze, folk get hyper.

Gran: They spilled oot inty The Walk, fists flying...
         What happened next, son – it was an *accident.*

Rab: I know that, Gran.

Gran: But efter the Hampden Riot the police just heard
         the words *Old Firm* and *Paddies* and *Jaffas...*

Rab: And put two and two together and got five.

Gran: Your da's never been the same since the jail. Your
         mum was the only thing that kept him straight.

Rab: Aye, he was always better when he was with her.

Gran: He just gave up efter she died.

Rab: I took wee Henky up to see him last week. We went
         to the park and that seemed to cheer Dad up.

Gran: Did wee Henky have his strip on?

Rab: Naw, Ania doesn't like him wearing it up the town.

Gran: Well that's a crying shame, when a wee boy can't
         wear his team colours wi' pride...

Rab: It's got to end somewhere, Gran and Ania wants it
         to end with him... Here, where's Weezee?

Gran: I thought she was at Eileen's...?

Rab: Naw, I sent her here. *Shite!* I'd better go find her.
         It's no' safe on The Walk today.

FISTS FLYING...

Robbie has arrived at his nan Mags Black's house. To his surprise, his mum, Karen, opens the door.

Robbie: Mum – I wasn't expecting to see you here...

Karen: Where else would I be? My boy's getting married!

Robbie: I know. I meant, *here,* at Nan's house.

Karen: Romeo wanted me here. So I'm here.

Robbie: Good. No, that's good... You look nice, Mum.

Karen: Thanks, son, you're looking well too.

Robbie: Shall we go in?

They go into the house. There is an awkward silence.

Robbie: How's, er... What's his name, again?

Karen: Eddy. He's well. He's a good man, Robbie.

Robbie: I'm glad. You deserve it, Mum.

Karen: And how's Rab? You boys still pals?

Robbie: Aye. He's doing well. He works for the council now.
         He's got a wee boy.

Karen: That's nice. He was a lovely lad. His gran did well,
         raising him alone after his ma died.

Robbie: She's still mad as a bag of hammers, but!

Karen: Aye, but she was there for him.

There is another long silence. The clock ticks. Karen sits on the sofa and starts to cry.

Karen: And *your* nan did a grand job looking after you, too,
         but I wish I'd taken you boys with me.

Robbie goes to his mum and comforts her.

Robbie: It's okay, Mum. We know what he did to you. You had to go.

Karen: I still have nightmares. Him coming home mortal. Reeking of drink and singing that bloody song.

Robbie: Aye – Dad still loves a chorus of 'The Sash'...

Karen: No, not that one. I never minded that one...

Robbie: *'Hullo, hullo, we are the Billy Boys.'*

Karen: Don't. Don't sing it, son. It tears me apart to think you were here, learning aw that hate.

Robbie: The song's banned now, Mum, and me an' Romeo never sang it anyway.

Karen: But your dad got you marching, eh?

Robbie: Aye, we went on the marches. It was fun when we were young. Felt good to belong to something.

Karen: I never wanted to belong to that. I never understood it – all that 'us' and 'them'.

Robbie: It's just history, Mum. And you know what they say about history? It's all in the past.

Karen: I wish that was true.

Robbie: The Battle of the Boyne was in 1690. I was born in 1993. Don't know about you – but I'm over it!

Karen laughs.

Karen: I see your nan painted the front door blue again.

Robbie: Aye, and the council will be round next week to paint it back...

Robbie's nan, Mags, arrives home. She sees Karen with Robbie.

Mags: So *you're* here are you?

Karen: I've come to see my boy married.

Mags: Well, I'll no' watch him marrying a McGowan.
         They're a bad lot and you know it.

Karen: I can see bad on both sides, Margaret.

Mags: And no doubt you've been telling Robbie here a pack
         of lies about his dad?

Robbie: I'm a grown man, I can make my own mind up.

Mags: You're a bairn and you know nothing!

Robbie: I know Romeo is getting married today and he wants
         you there.

Mags: I'll no' set foot in St Joseph's after what that
         mob did to this community. It tore us in two.

Robbie: A wedding might mend it. The way I hear it, both
         families had a hand in dividing The Walk.

Mags: The way you hear it? And what do you hear?

Robbie: What happened that cup final night.

Mags: Then you know what Mick McGowan did.

Robbie: I do, and he's paid for it. It's ruined his life.

Mags: At least he *had* a life.

Robbie: Nan, *everybody* says that dad started the fight.

Mags: Aye? Well they're all bloody liars...!

The Walk Inn May 10th 1980. Mags Black sits on a stool in a dark corner of the bar. Johnny stands by her, brooding.

Mags: See if she starts her singing, I'll belt her.

Johnny: She wouldn't dare, there's too many o' us in the bar tonight.

Gran saunters up.

Gran: Drowning your sorrows, Mags? Sounds like your mob started a right stooshie at Hampden.

Mags: It was your boy doing the fighting, Therese. My boy wasnae there, were you, Johnny?

Johnny: I've better things to do than watch a bunch of long-haired nancy boys have a kick about.

Mags: He was up at the Lodge, as it happens.

Gran: And what are you noo? A Grand Magician, is it?

Mags: Don't start Therese McGowan...

Gran: We'll no' be hearing 'The Sash' sung tonight, eh?

Johnny: Don't you worry, Mrs McGowan, we'll be singing it loud and proud on the twelfth.

Gran: Aye, but you dinnae come down The Walk...

Mags: Johnny has friends in high places. They've changed the route, Therese...

Johnny: So we'll be stopping by your house tae sing a rousing chorus – just for you.

Gran: Aye? Well I'm off to sing *my* favourite song. A wee salute to our victorious lads...

Mags: So help me, Johnny, I'll slap her smarmy pus.

Johnny: Don't worry, Ma... She'll no' sing for long.

Mags Black's house. Present Day. Robbie sits in the middle of an argument.

Mags: Mick McGowan was always rotten to the core!

Karen: He was no better nor worse than any of the lads on The Walk!

Robbie: Sandy Robertson says they were all pals back in the day – whatever their colours...

Mags: Mick got it from his dad. They say Old Man McGowan hud connections wi' the IRA.

Karen: And what did Johnny get from his dad, eh?

Mags: My husband was a fine, upstanding Protestant man. And so is my son!

Karen: Funny, I don't remember either of them going to church. It was never about religion, Margaret.

Mags: They are the *protectors* of our faith. Many a time was the Catholics would kill us for it!

Robbie: I know that, Nan. Like in France in the seventeenth century? But not *here* and *now*...

Mags: Are you being smart wi' me?

Karen: *He* has the benefit of a good education.

Mags: Don't you start. Is your boyfriend a Tim, eh? Always whining and asking for extra potatoes?

Robbie: Jesus, Nan – I'm sick o' this. I'm going out...

Mags: Ye canny run away from this family, Robbie. From who you *are!* Robbie...!

Robbie slams the door.

Mags: Whatever you think, Karen, I love your boys...

In a quiet wee corner of The Walk Romeo waits nervously by a tree bearing the legend 'Kylie + Romeo 4ever'. Kylie, wearing shades, pops her head around the tree.

Kylie: (*whispers urgently*) Romeo... Romeo.

Romeo: There you are!

Kylie: *Shush*! Oh Romeo... Romeo, why do you have to be a Black?

Romeo: Why do you have to be a McGowan?

Kylie: I'd do anything not to be right now.

Romeo: Me too. What a bloody mess. My nan's no' coming.

Kylie: Mine neither... and my brother's on the warpath.

Romeo: Aye, and my dad... Not that he deserves that name.

Kylie: Do you think it's all gonna kick off?

Romeo: I don't know... Disnae look good, but.

Kylie: This is supposed to be the happiest day of my life! What are we going to do?

Romeo: You want to call it off?

Kylie: No! I'd dye my hair, change my name and move to the Costa del Sol before I'd lose you...

Romeo: Don't be daft. Whatever your name, gorgeous, you'll always be the best girl in the town.

Kylie: I've got an idea. I'm off to see Father O'Brien. Meet me there in half an hour.

They kiss quickly and part ways. Weezee appears from behind another tree. She signs 'love' and gives us the thumbs up.

Kylie arrives at Father O'Brien's house. He is having tea with Reverend Scott.

O'Brien: Well hello, Kylie! Come away in. Do you know my friend, Reverend Scott?

Kylie: Aye, hello Reverend.

Scott: Please, call me Andrew... I thought you'd be in your big frock by now, Kylie?

Kylie: Me too, but it's no' really going to plan.

O'Brien: Oh dear, trouble in paradise? Where's young Romeo?

Kylie: On his way here. We're doing just fine. It's everybody else who's gone mental!

O'Brien: Is it St Joseph's that's the problem?

Scott: Because it's normal for the bride to choose...

Kylie: Nothing about our families is *normal*!

Kylie bursts into tears.

O'Brien: Oh now – this is supposed to be a happy day...

Kylie: I don't even like my *dress*. It makes me look like a toilet-roll holder...

Scott: Oh, I'm sure that's not true...

Kylie: And we just want to get married, we don't care where!

Scott: Well, I bet Father O'Brien and I can come up with an answer, can't we, Michael?

O'Brien: Of course we can, Andrew. We've won the Inter-faith Pub Quiz three years in a row, after all.

Robbie is charging along The Walk and barrels into Mr Levin with his messages, sending them flying.

Robbie: Aw sorry, Mr Levin. Let me get those...

Levin: Ocht, it's alright, son. I was hoping to bump into you, as it happens. Have you got a minute?

Robbie: Naw really... Actually, aye. What can I do for you? Your computer running okay?

Levin: Aye, it's grand, thanks, son. You were right. It's a great way to keep in touch wi' the family.

Robbie: Your son still oot in South Africa?

Levin: Aye, he says to ask you if you can get this Skype thing fer me? Says we can talk for free?

Robbie: I can set it up for you, aye. Maybe tomorrow?

Levin: That'll be fine, son. Me and my grandson are pals on Facebook now. He sends me all kinds of stuff.

Robbie: It can be good for that, aye.

Levin: He sent me a picture of an Israeli flag at a Rangers game? Is that right?

Robbie: Aye. And the Celtic Ultras have flown the Palestinian flag at matches.

Levin: Really? Why is this? Is this important to them?

Robbie: I don't know Mr L – they fly the Basque flag too and pictures of Che Guevara!

Levin: So they fly the flags in solidarity with other people?

Robbie: Maybe – or maybe it's because some of their own banners and songs have been banned?

WOOF!

ISRAEL

BASQUE

PALESTINE

CHÉ GUEVARA

Levin: So they just like to fly flags? But do they know what these flags mean to *other* people?

Robbie: I don't know, Mr Levin. The history of these countries is pretty complicated...

Levin: Very true – and I still canny see what this has got to do with playing football!

Robbie: If you ask me, it's just *some* fans finding a new way to noise each other up.

Levin: Ocht, there's already enough ways to turn the beautiful game into a dangerous game, son.

Robbie: Don't I know it.

Levin: Are you alright, son?

Robbie: Just ma family doin' ma head in.

Levin: Some families are complicated too.

Robbie: Aye and my nan is no' letting me forget it!

Levin: *Zachor* and *Shamor,* as my people say on our Sabbath. *Remember* and *Observe.*

Robbie: Is that Jewish, aye?

Levin: Aye, it's telling us to remember the history of our people and to celebrate our traditions.

Robbie: Does it tell you to destroy the traditions of other folk into the bargain? Or to hate them?

Levin: No, son, it does not.

Robbie: See ma problem is I'm loyal to my family but I don't like what they do in the name of 'loyalty'.

76

BELONGING
AND
IDENTITY

Karen is standing by Romeo and Kylie's tree. Johnny arrives.

Johnny: This used to be our place, mind? Back in the day.

Karen: Aye, the days before you'd use any excuse to get steamin' and use me as a punchbag.

Johnny: I'm very sorry for that, Kar. But I'm a changed man. I don't drink any more.

Karen: I'm sure you're a bloody saint...

Johnny: I'm a respectable member of this community, aye – with friends in high places.

Karen: And low ones too, no doubt.

Johnny: I'm no' here to start anything, Karen.

Karen: You don't need to – wi' your mother gunning for the whole McGowan tribe.

Johnny: She canny help feeling the way she does about that poor lad's murder.

Karen: I don't like it either but it was a bloody *accident*! And she didn't even know him!

Johnny: He was one of our boys, just the same.

Karen: So help me, Johnny, if you do anything to ruin Romeo's happiness, I'll ruin *you*...

Johnny: I'm just here to protect my family, that's aw.

Johnny walks off. He looks back and winks.

Johnny: My mother's decided to go, by the way. So we'll see you at the wedding, eh?

...SEE YOU AT THE WEDDING, EH?

Karen punches the tree in fury. Weezee comes out of hiding and tries to sneak by her.

Karen: Louise? Is that Wee Louise McGowan?

Weezee nods.

Karen: I don't know sign language, love. But you can lip-read, eh?

Weezee nods again.

Karen: Wish I was deaf after what I've heard today... Sorry, love – it's no' good being deaf is it?

Weezee signs something as Rab arrives.

Rab: She says, it's okay – she's got Spidey Senses.

Karen: Oh, like Spiderman, eh...? Hello, Rab.

Rab: Hello, Mrs Black.

Karen: It's Mrs White now, actually.

Rab: Naw? Really? That's magic. Robbie always said you and his dad were like black and white...

Karen: He's no' wrong. So how are you, Rab?

Rab: Hassled, to be honest. Gran heard old Mags is going to the wedding now, so she's going too.

Karen: There'll no' be a wedding at this rate!

Weezee signs to Rab.

Rab: Spiderman here says it'll all be fine... 'Mon you, we need to get home!

Karen: I'll see youse there, I hope.

The Black family are marching up The Walk to the church.

Karen: I don't understand why you're not at the church,
           Robbie...

Robbie: I told you, Mum. Romeo said he had something he had
           to do and to just come with you...

Karen: It's no' right. You're his best man. You should be
           with him. God, I hope he's okay.

Robbie: He'll be fine, Mum. Probably just needed some time
           to sort his head out.

Karen: Something feels wrong. What time is it?

Robbie: We've still got half an hour until it starts...

*Robbie's phone beeps. He's got a text. 'Meet me at the
tree'.*

Robbie: I'll see you there, okay, Mum?

Karen: Who's that texting you? Is it Romeo...?

Robbie takes off. Mags and Johnny catch up with Karen.

Mags: What's going on? Where's Robbie run off to?

Karen: Everything's fine, Margaret.

Mags: Oh, is that right? Where's Romeo, then? No one's
           seen him this past hour...

Johnny: Maybe he's seen the light and done a runner too?

Karen: Oh you'd like that, wouldn't you?

Johnny: You're the only one who wants to see him married to
           that wee bisum, Karen...

The McGowans are assembling outside Gran's house. Weezee comes out the house in her wedding outfit - including lace-up 'Wonder Woman' boots and a wee cape.

Gran: Louise McGowan, what are you wearing?

Rab: Aw, c'mon, Gran - she looks fine.

Gran: Go and change - I'll no give Mags Black an excuse to call us tinks.

Weezee signs to Rab.

Rab: Don't worry what it means, Weezee. It's no' a nice word and you shouldn't use it.

Gran: What? You canny say 'tinks' noo? What do you call them, then?

Rab: I think you mean 'Irish Travellers', Gran.

Gran: Ocht, the world's gone mad. I canny open ma mouth to speak any more.

Rab: Maybe that's a good thing, eh? If you don't like folk calling *you* names?

Ania: I think Weezee looks nice. Different, but nice.

Gran: Aye, well - you're foreign so what do you know?

Rab: Gran!

Eileen comes out the house.

Eileen: I don't feel right with Kylie not here...

Rab: I told you, she texted me. She says she just wants to talk to Father O'Brien before kick-off.

Eileen: But she doesn't know her dad's stuck on the rig.

Rab: I told Kylie *I'd* give her away if Uncle Jim
         couldn't make it.

The Blacks march past on the other side of The Walk.

Gran: Right, come on! I'm no' wanting that mob to get
         there before us...

Eileen: I don't care about them – I just want to know
         Kylie's alright...

Ania: See if anything starts, I'm packing my bags and me
         and Henky are moving to Edinburgh!

Rab: For Pete's sake, woman, I've told you – Edinburgh
         is just the same shit with different colours!

Ania: Don't you use that language in front of my son!

Rab: He's my son too, Ania, and like it or not this is
         his family.

Gran: Not until you pair get married, he's not. I'm
         telling you, you'll all end up in the hellfire...

Ania: Well, hell sounds like more fun than this!

Gran: Now listen here, you wee bisum...

Rab: Aw, knock it off both of you, would you?

Eileen: Something feels wrong. What time is it?

Rab: We've still got half an hour before it starts...
         Listen, I'll see you there okay?

Rab takes off. He's texting as he walks.

Eileen: Where are you going? Are you meeting Kylie...?

Ania: I mean it, Rab – NO TROUBLE OR I GO TO POLAND!

Gran: *Come on*, youse! Weezee, you'll have to do.

Rab is waiting by the 'family' tree. Robbie arrives.

Robbie: Are you alright, pal? Got your text...

Rab: Aye, just had to get away, like.

Robbie: Family doing your nut in, eh?

Rab: Totally... Don't suppose you've got a smoke?

Robbie: Naw, knocked it on the head.

Rab: Aye, me too. It's no' good when you've got a wean in the house.

Robbie: You're a good dad, Rab.

Rab: Well, I try to be, aye.

Robbie starts whistling 'Simply the Best'.

Rab: I hate that song.

Robbie: Aye, it's mince.

Rab: Gies me the shudders.

Robbie: Coz of the fitbaw?

Rab: Naw, man. Coz I remember my gran in a Tina Turner wig doing it at karaoke.

Robbie: (*whistles*) No' a pretty sight, eh?

Rab: It was her seventieth birthday party and she was wearing a miniskirt.

Robbie: Aw, man. Now I'll have nightmares.

Rab: Welcome to my world.

Robbie: It's banned on Radio Clyde, like. Coz it always starts a rammy.

Rab: Aye, I'm thinking we could get some other
          embarrassing songs banned too, like.

Robbie: Like 'Gangnam Style'?

Rab: Aye, man! That does ma heid in.

Robbie: You could make it a Celtic song, eh?

Rab: And you could sing it at Ibrox. Chuck in a wee
          FTP...

Robbie: Aye, and you change the lyrics 'n' aw... Doing it
          Celtic Style...

Rab: Both sides say it's *their* song...

Robbie: Banned fae the radio...

Rab: Never have to hear it again.

Robbie: Job done.

They laugh and shake hands.

Rab: Gonny naw tell that story about my gran, eh?

Rob: Naw, of course no'.

Rab: She's mental, but I canny let folk slag her off.

Robbie: I'm the same about my nan.

Rab: They're both mad, like... But we're okay, eh?

Robbie: So far, pal – so far.

Rab: Best get to the wedding then.

Robbie: Better had. I'll see you on the other side.

Rab: Man, this is shite.

Robbie: Aye, total shite.

The wedding guests are gathering outside St Joseph's.
Rab and Mr Levin stand with Weezee.

Levin: You're looking sharp, Louise. Like Wonder Woman.

Weezee signs to Rab.

Rab: She says thank you... And do you support
          Tottenham Hotspur?

Levin: Naw. Why would I? Aw... Because I'm a *Yid?*

Rab: I'm so sorry, Mr Levin – she doesn't know that's no'
          a nice word.

Levin: (*laughs*) Don't worry, I've been called worse than a
          Tottenham fan.

Rab: She's just seen people say it, like – she doesn't
          understand why they call themselves that.

Levin: Can't say I do either. You wouldn't want to be a
          'Yid' if you knew what happened to my family.

Rab: We do know, sir. We got taught about the Holocaust
          and the concentration camps in school.

Levin: You can learn from history, eh? It's good to
          remember where a wee bit of bigotry can lead to.

Rab: I'm sorry, Mr Levin. I'm pure mortified.

Levin: Forget it, Robert. It's just a name. *'A rose by any
          other name would smell as sweet.'*

Rab: *Romeo and Juliet* again? Did it no' go totally wrong
          for that pair *after* they got married?

Levin: That's a made-up story, son. This is the story of
          Romeo and Kylie and it'll have a happy ending.

Gran joins them, pointing over to where Mirembe, dressed in a bright orange African dress, is talking to Robbie.

Gran: Well now we know which side she's on. Will you *look* at that dress!

Rab: Mirembe's from Africa, Gran, no' Ulster.

Levin: I think she looks beautiful, myself.

He waves to Mirembe, who comes to join them.

Mirembe: Hullo, hullo! Well don't you all look *fine*!

Gran: Thank you. That's some dress you've got on.

Mirembe: Do you like it? It's traditional African fabric.

Gran: It's a very bright colour.

Mirembe: Oh, I *love* orange. Isn't it wonderful?

Gran: You wouldn't catch me wearing it, no.

Mirembe: But you could get away with it! You know, you remind me very much of *my* mother.

Gran: I don't see how.

Mirembe: You have both faced very difficult things in life and you are both very strong women.

Gran: I've had to be strong, aye.

Mirembe: My mother has had to be too. It shows you, eh? We're all the same, whatever our colour.

Levin: There are a lot of strong women on The Walk. They're very important to this community.

Mirembe: Yes, you and Mrs Black must be proud of your wonderful grandsons, Mrs McGowan.

Gran: Aye, well... I suppose so.

Father O'Brien comes out of the church.

Father: Rab, could you and Robbie do me a favour and gather everyone together?

ALL
COLOURS

The two families glare at each other as Father O'Brien addresses them. The Reverend stands by him.

Father: Good afternoon. Can I begin by saying how wonderful it is to see you all here...

Mags: Where's my grandson? Where's Romeo?

Gran: Done a runner, no doubt... Gutless toerag!

Father: If you could give me a moment to explain...

Mags: Well, I don't see your Kylie, either!

Father: I have a letter here...

Gran: No wonder – she'll be mortified!

Mags: Good! We all know Romeo can do better.

Gran: How dare you! You nasty wee...

Father: SHUT UP FOR ONE MINUTE!

There is a stunned silence.

Father: Apologies, ladies, but if you'll just *listen*... Romeo and Kylie came to see me an hour ago...

Gran: I knew it. The wedding's off.

Father: Not exactly. Reverend Scott and I both blessed their union and sent them on their way...

Mags: WHAT! This is all your fault, Therese McGowan!

Gran: My fault? How is it my fault?

Father: They asked me to read this letter to you...

Gran: I canny believe there'll be no wedding...!

Karen: For pity's sake – just let the man speak!

Father: '*Hullo everyone. We are very sorry we had to do this but we thought it would be better...*'

Mags: Poor Romeo, ashamed of his fiancée's family...

Father: '*We really wanted to get married but it was tearing our families apart...*'

Gran: It was the *Blacks* causing all the bother!

Father: '*So we decided to do this to avoid a rammy.*'

Mags: We would never have started anything!

Gran: Aw, you've been itching fer a fight!

Father: '*By the time you read this we'll be off to Las Vegas on our honeymoon...*'

Gran: You Blacks have always been free with your fists. Isn't that right, Karen?

Karen: Please leave me out of this.

Father: '*Where we'll get married by Elvis just to make sure it's well and truly done!*'

Gran: We all saw Karen's bruises after your son had a night on the town...

Mags: Well, maybe ma son has slapped his wife once or twice but he's no' a *murderer*!

Father: '*We are very happy and hope you can be happy for us too. Love from Romeo and Kylie.*'

Gran: It was an accident. Mick didn't mean it!

Mags: I saw him beating the daylights out of that boy!

Gran: They were *all* punching each other! All our lads were full of drink...

Mags: I'm sorry, Therese, but I know what I saw...

Gran: No one saw anything. No one saw the boy fall. No one saw him crack his head open.

Mags: That poor lad. It just broke my heart...

Gran: For crying out loud, Margaret, I'm a *mother*...!

Mags: Some mother!

Father: Ladies, *please!*

Mags: With a son who canny hold down a job and a grandson just out the jail...

Gran: Where he heard some tales about *Johnny Black*, I can tell you!

At this, Malkie slips away and starts to walk. Johnny sees him and starts walking too.

Mags: You're all scum, the lot of you!

Gran struggles to get to Mags.

Rab: Gran, stop. Let's just go...

Gran: To think a filthy Black was near the sacred altar of St Joseph's!

Robbie: That's enough, Mrs McGowan.

Mags: Who are you calling filthy, you dirty Paddy?

Rab: Tell your gran to shut it, Robbie.

Robbie: What did you say, McGowan?

Karen: Please boys – don't, *don't* start this... Father O'Brien, you'd better call the police!

Rab: You heard me, Robbie – shut her mouth or so help me, I'll do it for you.

Robbie: Come ahead, Rab... It is ON.

Karen: Stop – please, please STOP!

Malkie and Johnny are standing outside the church door. They eyeball each other – two cowboys ready to draw.

Malkie: Ready?

Johnny: Born ready, son. Let's go...

Suddenly Weezee – her cape flapping – comes flying up and throws herself between them. There is a scream and then deathly silence. After a few moments, the wail of sirens can be heard in the distance.

The next day. Mirembe and Mr Levin meet on The Walk.

Mirembe: It's terrible, just terrible. That poor little
            girl.

Levin: I canny quite believe it. I thought we put all
            this trouble behind us on The Walk.

Mirembe: I· knew the families didn't always get on but the
            boys, you know – such *nice* young men.

Levin: Aye, Rab and Robbie have never let their families
            spoil their friendship.

Mirembe: How will they get past this?

Levin: Maybe they won't and the trouble will never end.

Ania and Henky arrive.

Mirembe: Oh Ania – how are you? Is there any news?

Ania: Well, Weezee is out of surgery...

Levin: And...?

Ania: She is comfortable. They say she will be okay.

Mirembe: Thank God!

Ania: She is going to have scars, though. On her body
            and on her beautiful wee face.

Levin: Aw, the poor lassie.

Mirembe: But how, *how* did this happen?

Levin: Everybody was too busy screaming at each other to
            notice what was happening.

Ania: Aye – Weezee says she saw Malkie and Johnny leave
            and tried to tell everybody.

Levin: But nobody listened.

Ania: Nobody listened. So she decided to stop them by herself.

Levin: Like a wee superhero. She's the only person around here who really notices what's happening.

Mirembe: What a brave girl.

Levin: Do they know who did it, Ania?

Ania: The police say there were wounds from two different blades.

Levin: So Malcolm McGowan and Johnny Black were ready to kill each other.

Mirembe: For what? I just don't understand for what!

Ania: Neither do I, Mirembe.

Mirembe: When I came from Africa, I thought I was coming to a *safe* place.

Levin: You are safe, Mirembe. And so am I. We're in Scotland and this is *their* war, not ours.

Ania: It's not my war either and I don't want my son to be around here any more.

Levin: Are you leaving, Ania?

Ania: Aye. I told Rab if there was any trouble, I was going back to Poland.

Mirembe: What about Rab? Is he going with you?

Ania: I suppose he has to decide who he cares about the most – Henky and me or his mad family.

Rab is outside the old Walk Inn. It is all boarded up now and covered with sectarian graffiti from both sides. Rab sees us.

Rab: Why are you still here? Seen something you like? Naw – I didnae think so.

Robbie arrives. He sees us too.

Robbie: Come to have a gander at Scotland's shame, eh? Well, you can start with me...

Rab looks long and hard at Robbie. Robbie looks like he wants to run. But he doesn't.

Robbie: Bet you want to break ma nose again.

Rab: Aye – but I canny be bothered with another punny eccy. You looking for a brick to chuck?

Robbie: Naw – I'm shite at throwing. It was pure fluke I got you the first time, but.

Rab: True enough. I could always have you in a fight. What are you doing here, Robbie?

Robbie: Dunno – came to see where it all started, I suppose.

Rab: Don't kid yersel' – it didn't start wi' ma dad killing that boy. It started a *long* time ago.

Robbie: Aye, you're right and, listen, I'll never be talking to *ma* dad again.

Rab: Well, I'm no' exactly on speaking terms wi' ma cousin Malkie, either.

Robbie: Looks like they'll both get the jail.

Rab: You'll no' find me greetin' for them.

Robbie: Nor me. They took it too far.

Rab: They took it further – it had already gone too far.

Robbie: Aye, Nan is blaming herself, for once.

Rab: My gran's feeling pretty guilty too.

Robbie: I suppose we're all a wee bit guilty, eh? I mean,
        not *you*, but...

Rab: Don't worry, Rob – I know it's ma fault ma wee
        sister's in the hospital.

Robbie: Naw, it's no'. How were you to know what was gonnae
        happen?

Rab: We *saw* what was coming, Rob. We just didnae listen
        to ourselves.

Robbie: Except for Weezee. I've got something for her, by
        the way.

He hands Rab a book.

Rab: *Romeo and Juliet* – are you mad, like?

Robbie: Aye, she's maybe too young to understand it.

Rab: Don't be daft – she's the only one in ma family
        smart enough to understand it!

Robbie: Sorry, I just thought she'd like it. I can take
        it back.

Rab: Naw – it's nice. Leather cover and everything.

Robbie: Aye, it'll last. Maybe she can hand it down to her
        kids.

Rab: Aye, nice to hand down something *good*, eh?

Robbie: How's wee Henky doing, by the way?

Rab: Ania says she's taking him to Poland.

Robbie: Aw, shit...

Rab: Aye, and I've been saving up in secret for our wedding. I wanted to surprise her...

Robbie: That's awesome – I'd be there wi' bells on, pal! She'll stay for that, no?

Rab: Dunno. Says she doesn't *want* to go but canny stay on The Walk, like.

Robbie: How about somewhere else in Scotland, then? Somewhere quiet wi' no trouble.

Rab: Where's that, then?

Robbie: I dunno... Auchtermuchty?

Rab: Do they huv a football team?

Robbie: If they do it's probably a bit shite, eh?

Rab: Wonder what colour their strip would be?

Robbie: Tartan?

They laugh. There is a long silence.

Robbie: We widnae be Old Firm friends, then.

Rab: Naw, canny see how we could be, then. But I'm no' too sure how we can be *now*, either...

WHAT
HAPPENS
NEXT?

Walk The Walk – What Happens Next?

Discussion questions

1. What do you think will happen next?

2. What *could* happen next between these two families?

3. What *should* happen between these two families?

4. What should Ania do? Why?

5. What should Rab do? Why?

Now complete the activities below.

Follow-up discussion

1. As you read through *Walk The Walk*, what captured your attention or imagination (which character, storyline, scene)? Why?

2. In what ways does the book reflect people's real lives, identities, relationships and worlds?

3. In what ways does the book reflect your own experiences?

4. Have you learned anything from reading the book and/or completing the exercises?

5. Has the book made you think or feel differently about anything? If so, what, and why?

Photocopy this page for repeat use or print a copy from
www.scottishbooktrust.com/walkthewalk

Which column does each *Walk The Walk* character belong to at the end of the book?

What would they have to do in order to move into a more positive column?

Revenge	Uncertainty	Reconciliation	Forgiveness
Characters in the **revenge** column are angry, and want to punish the people they're angry with	Characters in the **uncertainty** column are not sure what they need to do	Characters in the **reconciliation** column want to make peace and feel remorse for their actions (they're sorry for what they did)	Characters in the **forgiveness** column are behaving in a way that promotes positive relationships

Rab should	Robbie should	Gran should
Mags should	Weezee should	Ania & Henky should
Romeo should	Kylie should	Malkie should
Johnny should	Karen should	Aunty Eileen should

Mr Levin should	Mirembe should	Father O'Brien should	Reverend Scott should

Photocopy this page for repeat use or print a copy from
www.scottishbooktrust.com/walkthewalk

Responsibility ladder: who is responsible for tackling sectarianism?

Place the following people on the ladder:

Me   My Friends   The Police   The Media
    People In My Community   Church Teachers/Educators
Councillors/The Provost   Celebrities   Footballers
        Football Clubs   Family   Politicians

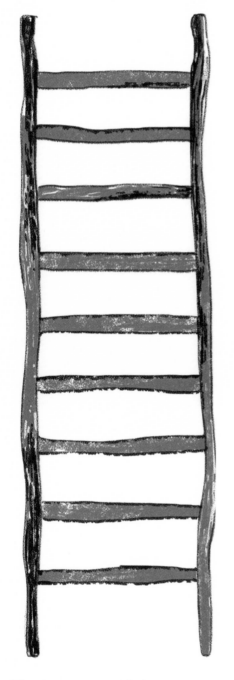

What could this person/these people do?
What could this person/these people do?
What could this person/these people do?
What could this person/these people do?
What could this person/these people do?
What could this person/these people do?
What could this person/these people do?
What could this person/these people do?
What could this person/these people do?

Glossary

a right soor pus	(Scots) a really grumpy face
a wee homer	(Scots) a small household chore or job, done for cash
Auchtermuchty	a town in Fife, Scotland
Bar-l	(slang) Barlinnie, Scotland's largest prison
Battle of the Boyne	a battle that took place in 1690 (*see Historical Context for more information*)
bairn	(Scots) baby or young child
bisum	(Scots) an unruly girl or woman
Bluenose	(slang) a fan of Rangers Football Club (FC)
Billy Boys	(slang) a term that some fans of Rangers FC use to describe themselves. 'The Billy Boys' is also a banned football chant
Bridezilla	(slang) a demanding bride-to-be
bromance	(slang) a bond between male friends
Bucky	(slang) Buckfast, a kind of fortified wine
Celtic Park	the home stadium of Celtic Football Club (FC)
Celts	(slang) fans of Celtic FC
chav	(slang) derogatory term for a brash person perceived to be lower class
Costa del Sol	a region in the south of Spain
done a runner	(slang) run away
doing your nut in	(slang) being annoying

fenian	(slang) a derogatory term for someone perceived to be a supporter of Irish nationalism
fife	woodwind instrument, like a flute
fitbaw	(Scots) football
FTP	(slang) F*** The Pope
gies me the shudders	(slang) makes me shudder
greetin'	(Scots) crying
gutless	(slang) cowardly
Hampden	Hampden Park, Scotland's national football stadium
have a gander	(slang) have a look
Heidy	Headteacher
Hunny	from *Hun* (slang), a Rangers FC fan
Ibrox	the home stadium of Rangers FC
IRA	Irish Republican Army (*see Historical Context for more information*)
it's mince	(Scots) it's rubbish
kura domowa	(Polish) housewife
Jaffas	(slang) *see Orange Men*
lassie	(Scots) young woman
messages	(Scots) grocery shopping
mono-blocking	a type of garden paving
mortal	(Scots) drunk
nearly got scalped	(slang) avoided a bad head injury

Old Firm	a collective name for Celtic and Rangers Football Clubs
Orange Men	members of the Orange Order (*see Historical Context for more information*)
Paddy	(slang) a derogatory term for an Irish person
Parkhead	the area of Glasgow where Celtic Park is located
Pete Tong	(rhyming slang) wrong
polis	(Scots) police
prodigal son	a person who rashly leaves their home, but then returns
punny eccy	(Scots) punishment exercise
rammy	(Scots) a fight
rig	offshore oil platform
Scotland's shame	a term sometimes used to describe sectarianism in Scotland
Shalom	Jewish word meaning *peace* or *peace be with you*. Also used instead of hello or goodbye
smarmy pus	(slang) smug face
steamin'	(slang) drunk
stooshie	(Scots) a fight
strip	football strip
Tap End or Bottom End	(slang) nicknames for different areas of the same town
the F word	see *fenian*
the Force	(slang) the police force

the Lodge	(slang) a Masonic Lodge, a meeting place for fraternal organisation the Freemasons
The Sash	short for 'The Sash My Father Wore', an Irish ballad sometimes sung by fans of Rangers FC
Tim	(slang) a fan of Celtic FC
tinks	(slang) a derogatory term for Irish or Scottish Travellers
toerag	(slang) a worthless person
Tottenham Hotspur	an English football club with a large Jewish following
Ulster	a province in Northern Ireland
wean	(Scots) small child
Yid	(slang) a derogatory term for a Jewish person. Also used to refer to fans of Tottenham Hotspur
youse	(slang) all of you
Zachor and Shamor	'remember' and 'observe', the two commandments of the Jewish Shabbat, or day of rest

Historical Context

The Battle of the Boyne was a battle fought in Ireland between William of Orange, who was Protestant, and James II, who was Catholic, in July 1690.

William of Orange's forces won a crushing victory in the battle. The Battle of the Boyne is still marked every 12th July in Scotland by, among other things, Orange Order marches.

For more information on the Battle of the Boyne, visit **www.bbc.co.uk/history/events/battle_of_the_boyne.**

The Orange Order is a fraternal organisation, named after William of Orange. On 12th July the 'Orange Men' march to commemorate the Battle of the Boyne.

The marchers carry banners and flags depicting Protestant symbols and scenes, such as William of Orange (also known as 'King Billy') crossing the Boyne.

To some Catholics, these marches feel sectarian, with some traditional Orange routes passing through or by Catholic areas. Efforts are made to reduce problems around contentious parades with re-routing and highly visible policing.

For more information on the Orange Order, visit **www.bbc.co.uk/news/uk-northern-ireland-18769781.**

The Irish Republican Army is also known as the IRA. It was founded nearly eighty years ago.

In 1969, the IRA split into the Official IRA and the Provisional IRA. When people now refer to the IRA, they nearly always mean the Provisional IRA.

The Provisional IRA wanted Northern Ireland to stop being part of the United Kingdom and become part of a united Ireland. In 1971 they began an offensive operation, which included bombings, to try to make this happen. A final ceasefire happened in July 1997, and the IRA agreed to give up all their weapons in 2005.

For more information on the IRA, visit **www.bbc.co.uk/history/recent/troubles/fact_files.shtml.**

Author's and Illustrator's Biographies

Gowan Calder is an actress, director and writer based in Scotland. She began her writing career as a playwright and her plays have been produced throughout the UK and broadcast on BBC Radio. Gowan was Writer in Residence in HMP Glenochil (2008–2009) and has run a variety of writing workshops within the Scottish Prison Service, as well as for youth theatres and adult writers' groups. From 2009 to 2011, she was Visiting Lecturer in Playwriting at Queen Margaret University, where she also worked with directing and acting students. She has enjoyed a long career as an actress since graduating with a degree in theatre in 1990. Her acting work has taken her around the world and from performing outdoors in a cloud of midges to recently filming *Teacup Travels* for CBeebies.

Gowan is the author of a previous book, *Skint!* – an interactive, graphic-novel-style exploration of money issues for young people, illustrated by Metaphrog. *Skint!* was published by Scottish Book Trust in 2011 and a further, revised edition was published in 2013 and reprinted in 2014.

Jill Calder is an award-winning illustrator and calligrapher with a love of drawing, ideas, colour, ink, typography, narrative, sketchbooks and, yes, deadlines. Jill blends traditional and digital image-making methods as seamlessly as possible to create whimsical narrative illustrations for an extraordinarily broad range of clients around the globe.

Jill trained at Edinburgh College of Art and later at Glasgow School of Art, graduating in 1992. Through her work, she has also been invited to teach at various schools and universities throughout the UK and also in Hong Kong.

Amongst other places, her work has been displayed at the V&A Museum, the National Museum of Scotland, the Royal Brompton Hospital and the Royal Scottish Academy.

Jill lives in Fife with her husband and two dogs.

Acknowledgements

We would like to acknowledge the following people and organisations for their support and guidance during the development of this book.

Steering group: Sophie Moxon, Deputy Director, Koren Calder, Young Adult Project Manager, Claire Askew, Young Adult Project Co-ordinator and Philippa Cochrane, Head of Reader Development, Scottish Book Trust; Vicki Burns, Campaign Manager, Show Racism The Red Card Scotland; Yvonne Donald, Tackling Sectarianism Development Officer, Education Scotland; Magi Gibson, Writer in Residence, Glasgow Women's Library; Alison Logan, Social Inclusion Officer, Sense Over Sectarianism; Russell McLarty, Storyteller with the Scottish Storytelling Forum, Mediator with Place for Hope and former Church of Scotland Parish Minister; Dermot Morrin, Honorary Roman Catholic Chaplain to the University of Edinburgh; Alette Willis, Chancellor's Fellow in the School of Health in Social Science, University of Edinburgh.

The *Walk The Walk* tutor support notes and learner activity ideas to accompany this book were created by Koren Calder, Young Adult Project Manager and Claire Askew, Young Adult Project Co-ordinator, Scottish Book Trust. www.scottishbooktrust.com/walkthewalk.

Advisors from the Voluntary Action Fund: Bill Weir, Programme Manager; Heather Wilkins and Joyce Munro, Programme Development Officers.

Advisors from other Tackling Sectarianism-funded projects: Peter Johnson, Stand Up To Sectarianism Senior Development Worker, Youth Scotland; George McGowan, Anti-Sectarianism Project and Training Development Worker, Deaf Connections; Julia Rodriguez Nieto, Project Co-ordinator, XChange Scotland; Rachel Thain-Gray, 'Mixing The Colours' Project Development Worker, Glasgow Women's Library.

Literacy support groups involved in the development of *Walk The Walk*

Adult Basic Education at Bathgate staff: Scott Duguid, Joe Gallagher. **Learners:** Sean Donohoe, Kevin Farquhar, Ryan Fullerton, Danny Parkes, Jay Schumacher and Paul.

Care Leavers Employment Service at Glasgow Kelvin College: Catherine Campbell, Amanda McLauchlan and learners from the Core Skills programme.

Entry to Learning at Edinburgh College (Granton) staff: Fiona Waterston, Gerry Forsyth. **Learners:** Hamish Bowes, Jack Browning, Ian Campbell, Harry Mackinnon, Alex Mavor, Callum Smith, Hamza Tariq, Robson Thorburn.

Glasgow Clyde College Creative Writing group at the Whiteinch Centre staff: Anne-Marie Timoney. **Learners:** Tanya Coyle, Chris Martin, Alan McDonald, Michael Kerins, Adam Paxton, Pardeep Saran, David Shannon.

Glory and Dismay at Hearts FC Community Trust staff: Kenny Fyfe, James Gilfillan, Hazel Lyons, Nicol McCrossan, John Player, John Semple. **Learners:** John Maclean Abercrombie, Tuesday Burgess, Richard Carr, Mark Couper, Charlie Farrell, John Gibson, Eric Hogg, Suzie Johnston, Gerry McKenna, Chris Rankin, Laura Thomson, George White.

Prince's Trust Team 42 at Glasgow Clyde College (Cardonald) staff: Thomas Walker. **Learners:** Chelsea Hannah, Caitlin Keith, Sharee Lynn, Caitlin McManus, Kimberley Morrison, James Webster.

Oban High School, Oban Library Readers Group, Oban WoodWord group, 1:1 learners and tutors, and Oban Youth Café staff: Brian Marden, Leonie Charlton, Scott Douglas, Marian Eydmann, Colin Johnson, Rosaleen Laverty, Catriona Smith, Janie Steele. **Learners:** Ross Cameron, Christine Carmichael, Lyndsay Foster, Gary Gemmell, John Robert Gibson, Emma MacDougall, Peter Miller, Mhairi Scott, Lorraine Smith.

Redburn Youth Centre Activity Agreement Group staff: Ricky Caig, Jennifer Haining, Kenny Harrow, Maureen Meechan, Kieran Morrell. **Learners:** Stephen Becket, Declan Bell, Thomas Dempsey, Beth Doherty, Jack Frew, Rebecca Kerr, Hayley McCann, Nadine McConville, Jordan Nicol, Levi Thomson, Demi Turner, Emma Walker.

South Ayrshire Youth Forum staff: Brian Borland. **Learners:** Aiden Anderson, Kate Fleming, Kai Green, Craig Hamilton, Mason Rowan.

The Welcoming Project, Scotland for Newcomers staff: Tuesday Burgess, Jon Busby, Hazel Lyons. **Learners:** Panos Bantzis, Sidra Bellorini, Natalia Benitez, Sara Bueno, Silvia Dobroviceanu, Thomas Duda, Janina Grosse, Carolina Jimenez-Jorres, Eunhee Lee, Thibaut Nkulikiyimana, Elena Perez, Gabriel Salva, Rocio Villa.